EPICURUS

EPICURUS

Essential Epicurus

TOP 10
World

THE BIG NEST

THE BIG NEST

LONDON · NEW YORK · TORONTO · SAO PAULO · MOSCOW
PARIS · MADRID · BERLIN · ROME · MEXICO CITY · MUMBAI · SEOUL · DOHA
TOKYO · SYDNEY · CAPE TOWN · AUCKLAND · BEIJING

New Edition

Published by The Big Nest

This Edition first published in 2018

ISBN: 9781787246867

CONTENTS

PRINCIPAL DOCTRINES

1. A happy and eternal being has no trouble himself and brings no trouble upon any other being; hence he is exempt from movements of anger and partiality, for every such movement implies weakness

2. Death is nothing to us; for the body, when it has been resolved into its elements, has no feeling, and that which has no feeling is nothing to us.

3. The magnitude of pleasure reaches its limit in the removal of all pain. When pleasure is present, so long as it is uninterrupted, there is no pain either of body or of mind or of both together.

4. Continuous pain does not last long in the body; on the contrary, pain, if extreme, is present a short time, and even that degree of pain which barely outweighs pleasure in the body does not last for many days together. Illnesses of long duration even permit of an excess of pleasure over pain in the body.

5. It is impossible to live a pleasant life without living wisely and well and justly, and it is impossible to live wisely and well and justly without living pleasantly. Whenever any one of these is lacking, when, for instance, the person is not able to live wisely, though he lives well and justly, it is impossible for him to live a pleasant life.

6. In order to obtain security from other people any means whatever of procuring this was a natural good.

7. Some people have sought to become famous and renowned, thinking that thus they would make themselves

secure against their fellow-humans. If, then, the life of such persons really was secure, they attained natural good; if, however, it was insecure, they have not attained the end which by nature's own prompting they originally sought.

8. No pleasure is in itself evil, but the things which produce certain pleasures entail annoyances many times greater than the pleasures themselves.

9. If all pleasure had been capable of accumulation, – if this had gone on not only be recurrences in time, but all over the frame or, at any rate, over the principal parts of human nature, there would never have been any difference between one pleasure and another, as in fact there is.

10. If the objects which are productive of pleasures to profligate persons really freed them from fears of the mind, – the fears, I mean, inspired by celestial and atmospheric phenomena, the fear of death, the fear of pain; if, further, they taught them to limit their desires, we should never have any fault to find with such persons, for they would then be filled with pleasures to overflowing on all sides and would be exempt from all pain, whether of body or mind, that is, from all evil.

11. If we had never been molested by alarms at celestial and atmospheric phenomena, nor by the misgiving that death somehow affects us, nor by neglect of the proper limits of pains and desires, we should have had no need to study natural science.

12. It would be impossible to banish fear on matters of the highest importance, if a person did not know the nature of the whole universe, but lived in dread of what the legends tell us. Hence without the study of nature there was no enjoyment of unmixed pleasures.

13. There would be no advantage in providing security

against our fellow humans, so long as we were alarmed by occurrences over our heads or beneath the earth or in general by whatever happens in the boundless universe.

14. When tolerable security against our fellow humans is attained, then on a basis of power sufficient to afford supports and of material prosperity arises in most genuine form the security of a quiet private life withdrawn from the multitude.

15. Nature's wealth at once has its bounds and is easy to procure; but the wealth of vain fancies recedes to an infinite distance.

16. Fortune but seldom interferes with the wise person; his greatest and highest interests have been, are, and will be, directed by reason throughout the course of his life.

17. The just person enjoys the greatest peace of mind, while the unjust is full of the utmost disquietude.

18. Pleasure in the body admits no increase when once the pain of want has been removed; after that it only admits of variation. The limit of pleasure in the mind, however, is reached when we reflect on the things themselves and their congeners which cause the mind the greatest alarms.

19. Unlimited time and limited time afford an equal amount of pleasure, if we measure the limits of that pleasure by reason.

20. The body receives as unlimited the limits of pleasure; and to provide it requires unlimited time. But the mind, grasping in thought what the end and limit of the body is, and banishing the terrors of futurity, procures a complete and perfect life, and has no longer any need of unlimited time. Nevertheless it does not shun pleasure, and even in the hour of death, when ushered out of existence by circumstances, the mind does not lack enjoyment

of the best life.

21. He who understands the limits of life knows how easy it is to procure enough to remove the pain of want and make the whole of life complete and perfect. Hence he has no longer any need of things which are not to be won save by labor and conflict.

22. We must take into account as the end all that really exists and all clear evidence of sense to which we refer our opinions; for otherwise everything will be full of uncertainty and confusion.

23. If you fight against all your sensations, you will have no standard to which to refer, and thus no means of judging even those judgements which you pronounce false.

24. If you reject absolutely any single sensation without stopping to discriminate with respect to that which awaits confirmation between matter of opinion and that which is already present, whether in sensation or in feelings or in any immediate perception of the mind, you will throw into confusion even the rest of your sensations by your groundless belief and so you will be rejecting the standard of truth altogether. If in your ideas based upon opinion you hastily affirm as true all that awaits confirmation as well as that which does not, you will not escape error, as you will be maintaining complete ambiguity whenever it is a case of judging between right and wrong opinion.

25. If you do not on every separate occasion refer each of your actions to the end prescribed by nature, but instead of this in the act of choice or avoidance swerve aside to some other end, your acts will not be consistent with your theories.

26. All such desires as lead to no pain when they remain ungratified are unnecessary, and the longing is easily

got rid of, when the thing desired is difficult to procure or when the desires seem likely to produce harm.

27. Of all the means which are procured by wisdom to ensure happiness throughout the whole of life, by far the most important is the acquisition of friends.

28. The same conviction which inspires confidence that nothing we have to fear is eternal or even of long duration, also enables us to see that even in our limited conditions of life nothing enhances our security so much as friendship.

29. Of our desires some are natural and necessary others are natural, but not necessary; others, again, are neither natural nor necessary, but are due to illusory opinion.

30. Those natural desires which entail no pain when not gratified, though their objects are vehemently pursued, are also due to illusory opinion; and when they are not got rid of, it is not because of their own nature, but because of the person's illusory opinion.

31. Natural justice is a symbol or expression of usefulness, to prevent one person from harming or being harmed by another.

32. Those animals which are incapable of making covenants with one another, to the end that they may neither inflict nor suffer harm, are without either justice or injustice. And those tribes which either could not or would not form mutual covenants to the same end are in like case.

33. There never was an absolute justice, but only an agreement made in reciprocal association in whatever localities now and again from time to time, providing against the infliction or suffering of harm.

34. Injustice is not in itself an evil, but only in its consequence, viz. the terror which is excited by apprehension that those appointed to punish such offenses will discover

the injustice.

35. It is impossible for the person who secretly violates any article of the social compact to feel confident that he will remain undiscovered, even if he has already escaped ten thousand times; for right on to the end of his life he is never sure he will not be detected.

36. Taken generally, justice is the same for all, to wit, something found useful in mutual association; but in its application to particular cases of locality or conditions of whatever kind, it varies under different circumstances.

37. Among the things accounted just by conventional law, whatever in the needs of mutual association is attested to be useful, is thereby stamped as just, whether or not it be the same for all; and in case any law is made and does not prove suitable to the usefulness of mutual association, then this is no longer just. And should the usefulness which is expressed by the law vary and only for a time correspond with the prior conception, nevertheless for the time being it was just, so long as we do not trouble ourselves about empty words, but look simply at the facts.

38. Where without any change in circumstances the conventional laws, when judged by their consequences, were seen not to correspond with the notion of justice, such laws were not really just; but wherever the laws have ceased to be useful in consequence of a change in circumstances, in that case the laws were for the time being just when they were useful for the mutual association of the citizens, and subsequently ceased to be just when they ceased to be useful.

39. He who best knew how to meet fear of external foes made into one family all the creatures he could; and those he could not, he at any rate did not treat as aliens; and

where he found even this impossible, he avoided all association, and, so far as was useful, kept them at a distance.

40. Those who were best able to provide themselves with the means of security against their neighbours, being thus in possession of the surest guarantee, passed the most agreeable life in each other's society; and their enjoyment of the fullest intimacy was such that, if one of them died before his time, the survivors did not mourn his death as if it called for sympathy.

VATICAN SAYINGS

QUOTES OF EPICURUS AND OTHER EPICUREANS
PRESERVED IN A 14TH CENTURY MANUSCRIPT FROM
THE VATICAN LIBRARY

1. (PD 1) A blessed and indestructible being has no trouble himself and brings no trouble upon any other being; so he is free from anger and partiality, for all such things imply weakness.

2. (PD 2) Death is nothing to us; for that which has been dissolved into its elements experiences no sensations, and that which has no sensation is nothing to us.

3. (PD 4) Continuous bodily pain does not last long; instead, pain, if extreme, is present a very short time, and even that degree of pain which slightly exceeds bodily pleasure does not last for many days at once. Diseases of long duration allow an excess of bodily pleasure over pain.

4. Every pain is easy to disregard; for that which is intense is of brief duration, and those bodily pains that last long are mild.

5. (PD 5) It is impossible to live a pleasant life without living wisely and honorably and justly, and it is impossible to live wisely and honorably and justly without living pleasantly. Whenever any one of these is lacking, when, for instance, the man is not able to live wisely, though he lives honorably and justly, it is impossible for him to live a pleasant life.

6. (PD 35) It is impossible for a man who secretly violates the terms of the agreement not to harm or be harmed

to feel confident that he will remain undiscovered, even if he has already escaped ten thousand times; for until his death he is never sure that he will not be detected.

7. For an aggressor to be undetected is difficult; and for him to be confident that his concealment will continue is impossible.

8. (PD 15) The wealth required by nature is limited and is easy to procure; but the wealth required by vain ideals extends to infinity.

9. Necessity is an evil; but there is no necessity for continuing to live with necessity.

10. Remember that you are mortal and have a limited time to live and have devoted yourself to discussions on nature for all time and eternity and have seen "things that are now and are to me come and have been."

11. Most men are insensible when they rest, and mad when they act.

12. (PD 17) The just man is most free from disturbance, while the unjust is full of the utmost disturbance.

13. (PD 37) Among the things held to be just by law, whatever is proved to be of advantage in men's dealings has the stamp of justice, whether or not it be the same for all; but if a man makes a law and it does not prove to be mutually advantageous, then this is no longer just. And if what is mutually advantageous varies and only for a time corresponds to our concept of justice, nevertheless for that time it is just for those who do not trouble themselves about empty words, but look simply at the facts.

14. We have been born once and cannot be born a second time; for all eternity we shall no longer exist. But you, although you are not in control of tomorrow, are postponing your happiness. Life is wasted by delaying, and each

one of us dies without enjoying leisure.

15. We place a high value on our characters as if they were our own possessions whether or not we are virtuous and praised by other men. So, too, we must regard the characters of those around us if they are our friends.

16. No one chooses a thing seeing that it is evil; but being lured by it when it appears good in comparison to a greater evil, he is caught.

17. We should not view the young man as happy, but rather the old man whose life has been fortunate. The young man at the height of his powers is often befuddled by chance and driven from his course; but the old man has dropped anchor in old age as in a harbor, since he secures in sure and thankful memory goods for which he was once scarcely confident of.

18. If sight, association, and intercourse are removed, the passion of love is ended.

19. He has become an old man on the day on which he forgot his past blessings.

20. (PD 29) Of our desires some are natural and necessary, others are natural but not necessary; and others are neither natural nor necessary, but are due to groundless opinion.

21. We must not force Nature but persuade her. We shall persuade her if we satisfy the necessary desires and also those bodily desires that do not harm us while sternly rejecting those that are harmful.

22. (PD 19) Unlimited time and limited time afford an equal amount of pleasure, if we measure the limits of that pleasure by reason.

23. Every friendship in itself is to be desired; but the initial cause of friendship is from its advantages.

24. Dreams have neither a divine nature nor a prophetic power, but they are the result of images that impact on us.

25. Poverty, if measured by the natural end, is great wealth; but wealth, if not limited, is great poverty.

26. One must presume that long and short arguments contribute to the same end.

27. The benefits of other activities come only to those who have already become, with great difficulty, complete masters of such pursuits, but in the study of philosophy pleasure accompanies growing knowledge; for pleasure does not follow learning; rather, learning and pleasure advance side by side.

28. Those who are overly eager to make friends are not to be approved; nor yet should you approve those who avoid friendship, for risks must be run for its sake.

29. To speak frankly as I study nature I would prefer to speak in oracles that which is of advantage to all men even though it be understood by none, rather than to conform to popular opinion and thus gain the constant praise that comes from the many.

30. Some men spend their whole life furnishing for themselves the things proper to life without realizing that at our birth each of us was poured a mortal brew to drink.

31. It is possible to provide security against other things, but as far as death is concerned, we men all live in a city without walls.

32. The honor paid to a wise man is itself a great good for those who honor him.

33. The cry of the flesh is not to be hungry, thirsty, or cold; for he who is free of these and is confident of remain so might vie even with Zeus for happiness.

34. We do not so much need the assistance of our

friends as we do the confidence of their assistance in need.

35. Don't spoil what you have by desiring what you don't have; but remember that what you now have was once among the things only hoped for.

36. Epicurus's life when compared to that of other men with respect to gentleness and self-sufficiency might be thought a mere legend.

37. When confronted by evil nature is weak, but not when faced with good; for pleasures make it secure but pains ruin it.

38. He is of very small account for whom there are many good reasons for ending his life.

39. Neither he who is always seeking material aid from his friends nor he who never considers such aid is a true friend; for one engages in petty trade, taking a favor instead of gratitude, and the other deprives himself of hope for the future.

40. He who asserts that everything happens by necessity can hardly find fault with one who denies that everything happens by necessity; by his own theory this very argument is voiced by necessity.

41. At one and the same time we must philosophize, laugh, and manage our household and other business, while never ceasing to proclaim the words of true philosophy.

42. The same time produces both the beginning of the greatest good and the dissolution of the evil.

43. The love of money, if unjustly gained, is impious, and, if justly, shameful; for it is inappropriate to be miserly even with justice on one's side.

44. The wise man who has become accustomed to necessities knows better how to share with others than how to take from them, so great a treasure of self-sufficiency

has he found.

45. The study of nature does not create men who are fond of boasting and chattering or who show off the culture that impresses the many, but rather men who are strong and self-sufficient, and who take pride in their own personal qualities not in those that depend on external circumstances.

46. Let us completely rid ourselves of our bad habits as if they were evil men who have done us long and grievous harm.

47. I have anticipated you, Fortune, and entrenched myself against all your secret attacks. And we will not give ourselves up as captives to you or to any other circumstance; but when it is time for us to go, spitting contempt on life and on those who here vainly cling to it, we will leave life crying aloud in a glorious triumph-song that we have lived well.

48. While we are on the road, we must try to make what is before us better than what is past; when we come to the road's end, we feel a smooth contentment.

49. (PD 12) It is impossible for someone to dispel his fears about the most important matters if he doesn't know the nature of the universe but still gives some credence to myths. So without the study of nature there is no enjoyment of pure pleasure.

50. (PD 8) No pleasure is a bad thing in itself, but the things which produce certain pleasures entail disturbances many times greater than the pleasures themselves.

51. [addressing a young man] I understand from you that your natural disposition is too much inclined toward sexual passion. Follow your inclination as you will, provided only that you neither violate the laws, disturb

well-established customs, harm any one of your neighbors, injure your own body, nor waste your possessions. That you be not checked by one or more of these provisos is impossible; for a man never gets any good from sexual passion, and he is fortunate if he does not receive harm.

52. Friendship dances around the world bidding us all to awaken to the recognition of happiness.

53. We must envy no one; for the good do not deserve envy and as for the bad, the more they prosper, the more they ruin it for themselves.

54. It is not the pretense but the real pursuit of philosophy that is needed; for we do not need the semblance of health but rather true health.

55. We should find solace for misfortune in the happy memory of what has been and in the knowledge that what has been cannot be undone.

56–57. The wise man feels no more pain when being tortured himself than when his friend tortured, and will die for him; for if he betrays his friend, his whole life will be confounded by distrust and completely upset.

58. We must free ourselves from the prison of public education and politics.

59. What cannot be satisfied is not a man's stomach, as most men think, but rather the false opinion that the stomach requires unlimited filling.

60. Every man passes out of life as if he had just been born.

61. Most beautiful is the sight of those close to us, when our original contact makes us of one mind or produces a great incitement to this end.

62. If the anger of parents against their children is justified, it is quite pointless for the children to resist it and

to fail to ask forgiveness. If the anger is not justified but is unreasonable, it is folly for an irrational child to appeal to someone deaf to appeals and not to try to turn it aside in other directions by a display of good will.

63. There is also a limit in simple living, and he who fails to understand this falls into an error as great as that of the man who gives way to extravagance.

64. We should welcome praise from others if it comes unsought, but we should be concerned with healing ourselves.

65. It is pointless for a man to pray to the gods for that which he has the power to obtain by himself.

66. We show our feeling for our friends' suffering, not with laments, but with thoughtful concern.

67. Since the attainment of great wealth can scarcely be accomplished without slavery to crowds or to politicians, a free life cannot obtain much wealth; but such a life already possesses everything in unfailing supply. Should such a life happen to achieve great wealth, this too it can share so as to gain the good will of one's neighbors.

68. Nothing is enough to someone for whom what is enough is little.

69. The thankless nature of the soul makes the creature endlessly greedy for variations in its lifestyle.

70. Do nothing in your life that will cause you to fear if it is discovered by your neighbor.

71. Question each of your desires: "What will happen to me if that which this desire seeks is achieved, and what if it is not?"

72. (PD 13) There is no advantage to obtaining protection from other men so long as we are alarmed by events above or below the earth or in general by whatever happens

in the boundless universe.

73. That we have suffered certain bodily pains aids us in preventing others like them.

74. In a philosophical dispute, he gains most who is defeated, since he learns the most.

75. The saying, "look to the end of a long life," shows small thanks for past good fortune.

76. As you grow old you are such as I urge you to be, and you have recognized the difference between studying philosophy for yourself and studying it for Greece. I rejoice with you.

77. Freedom is the greatest fruit of self-sufficiency.

78. The noble man is chiefly concerned with wisdom and friendship; of these, the former is a mortal good, the latter an immortal one.

79. He who is calm disturbs neither himself nor another.

80. The first step towards salvation is to attend to one's youth and guard against that which defiles everything through maddening desires.

81. The soul neither rids itself of disturbance nor gains a worthwhile joy through the possession of greatest wealth, nor by the honor and admiration bestowed by the crowd, or through any of the other things sought by unlimited desire.

LETTER TO MENOECEUS

ABOUT ETHICS

Greetings:

Let no one be slow to seek wisdom when he is young nor weary in the search thereof when he is grown old. For no age is too early or too late for the health of the soul. And to say that the season for studying philosophy has not yet come, or that it is past and gone, is like saying that the season for happiness is not yet or that it is now no more. Therefore, both old and young ought to seek wisdom, the former in order that, as age comes over him, he may be young in good things because of the grace of what has been, and the latter in order that, while he is young, he may at the same time be old, because he has no fear of the things which are to come. So we must exercise ourselves in the things which bring happiness, since, if that be present, we have everything, and, if that be absent, all our actions are directed toward attaining it.

Those things which without ceasing I have declared to you, those do, and exercise yourself in those, holding them to be the elements of right life. First believe that God is a living being immortal and happy, according to the notion of a god indicated by the common sense of humankind; and so of him anything that is at agrees not with about him whatever may uphold both his happiness and his immortality. For truly there are gods, and knowledge of them is evident; but they are not such as the multitude believe, seeing that people do not steadfastly maintain the notions they form respecting them. Not the person who denies the gods worshipped by the multitude, but he who affirms of the gods what the multitude believes about them is truly impious. For the utterances of the multitude about the gods are not true preconceptions but false assumptions; hence it is that the greatest evils happen to the wicked and the greatest blessings happen to the good from the hand of the gods, seeing that they are always favourable to their own good qualities and take pleasure in people like to themselves, but reject as alien whatever is not of their kind.

Accustom yourself to believe that death is nothing to us, for good and evil imply awareness, and death is the privation of all awareness; therefore a right understanding that death is nothing to us makes the mortality of life enjoyable, not by adding to life an unlimited time, but by taking away the yearning after immortality. For life has no terror; for those who thoroughly apprehend that there are no terrors for them in ceasing to live. Foolish, therefore, is the person who says that he fears death, not because it will pain when it comes, but because it pains in the prospect. Whatever causes no annoyance when it is present, causes only a groundless pain in the expectation. Death, therefore, the most awful of evils, is nothing to us, seeing that, when we are, death is not come, and, when death is come, we are not. It is nothing, then, either to the living or to the dead, for with the living it is not and the dead exist no longer. But in the world, at one time people shun death as the greatest of all evils, and at another time choose it as a respite from the evils in life. The wise person does not deprecate life nor does he fear the cessation of life. The thought of life is no offense to him, nor is the cessation of life regarded as an evil. And even as people choose of food not merely and simply the larger portion, but the more pleasant, so the wise seek to enjoy the time which is most pleasant and not merely that which is longest. And he who admonishes the young to live well and the old to make a good end speaks foolishly, not merely because of the desirability of life, but because the same exercise at once teaches to live well and to die well. Much worse is he who says that it were good not to be born, but when once one is born to pass with all speed through the gates of Hades. For if he truly believes this, why does he not depart from life? It were easy for him to do so, if once he were firmly convinced. If he speaks only in mockery, his words are foolishness, for those who hear believe him not.

We must remember that the future is neither wholly ours nor wholly not ours, so that neither must we count upon it as quite certain to come nor despair of it as quite certain not to come.

We must also reflect that of desires some are natural, others are groundless; and that of the natural some are necessary as well as natural, and some natural only. And of the necessary desires some are necessary if we are to be happy, some if the body is to be rid of uneasiness, some if we are even to live. He who has a clear and certain understanding of these things will direct every preference and aversion toward securing health of body and tranquillity of mind, seeing that this is the sum and end of a happy life. For the end of all our actions is to be free from pain and fear, and, when once we have attained all this, the tempest of the soul is laid; seeing that the living creature has no need to go in search of something that is lacking, nor to look anything else by which the good of the soul and of the body will be fulfilled. When we are pained pleasure, then, and then only, do we feel the need of pleasure. For this reason we call pleasure the alpha and omega of a happy life. Pleasure is our first and kindred good. It is the starting-point of every choice and of every aversion, and to it we come back, inasmuch as we make feeling the rule by which to judge of every good thing. And since pleasure is our first and native good, for that reason we do not choose every pleasure whatever, but often pass over many pleasures when a greater annoyance ensues from them. And often we consider pains superior to pleasures when submission to the pains for a long time brings us as a consequence a greater pleasure. While therefore all pleasure because it is naturally akin to us is good, not all pleasure is worthy of choice, just as all pain is an evil and yet not all pain is to be shunned. It is, however, by measuring one against another, and by looking at the conveniences and inconveniences, teat all these matters must be judged. Sometimes we treat the good as an evil, and the evil, on the contrary, as a good. Again, we regard independence of outward things as a great good, not so as in all cases to use little, but so as to be contented with little if we have not much, being honestly persuaded that they have the sweetest enjoyment of luxury who stand least in need of it, and that whatever is natural is easily procured and only the vain and worthless hard to win. Plain fare gives as much pleasure as a costly diet, when one the pain of want has been removed, while bread an water confer the highest possible pleasure when they are brought to hungry lips. To habituate one's se therefore, to simple and inexpensive diet supplies al that is needful for health, and enables a person to meet the necessary requirements of life without shrinking and it places us in a better condition when we approach at intervals a costly fare and renders us fearless of fortune.

When we say, then, that pleasure is the end and aim, we do not mean the pleasures of the prodigal or the pleasures of sensuality, as we are understood to do by some through ignorance, prejudice, or wilful misrepresentation. By pleasure we mean the absence of pain in the body and of trouble in the soul. It is not an unbroken succession of drinking-bouts and of merrymaking, not sexual love, not the enjoyment of the fish and other delicacies of a luxurious table, which produce a pleasant life; it is sober reasoning, searching out the grounds of every choice and avoidance, and banishing those beliefs through which the greatest disturbances take possession of the soul. Of all this the d is prudence. For this reason prudence is a more precious thing even than the other virtues, for ad a life of pleasure which is not also a life of prudence, honour, and justice; nor lead a life of prudence, honour, and justice, which is not also a life of pleasure. For the virtues have grown into one with a pleasant life, and a pleasant life is inseparable from them.

Who, then, is superior in your judgment to such a person? He holds a holy belief concerning the gods, and is altogether free from the fear of death. He has diligently considered the end fixed by nature, and understands how easily the limit of good things can be reached and attained, and how either the duration or the intensity of evils is but slight. Destiny which some introduce as sovereign over all things, he laughs to scorn, affirming rather that some things happen of necessity, others by chance, others through our own agency. For he sees that necessity destroys responsibility and that chance or fortune is inconstant; whereas our own actions are free, and it is to them that praise and blame naturally attach. It were better, indeed, to accept the legends of the gods than to bow beneath destiny which the natural philosophers have imposed. The one holds out some faint hope that we may escape if we honour the gods, while the necessity of the naturalists is deaf to all entreaties. Nor does he hold chance to be a god, as the world in general does, for in the acts of a god there is no disorder; nor to be a cause, though an uncertain one, for he believes that no good or evil is dispensed by chance to people so as to make life happy, though it supplies the starting-point of great good and great evil. He believes that the misfortune of the wise is better than the prosperity of the fool. It is better, in short, that what is well judged in action should not owe its successful issue to the aid of chance.

Exercise yourself in these and kindred precepts day and night, both by yourself and with him who is like to you; then never, either in waking or in dream, will you be disturbed, but will live as a god among people. For people lose all appearance of mortality by living in the midst of immortal blessings.

LETTER TO HERODOTUS

ABOUT NATURE AND HAPPINESS

Greetings:

For those who are unable to study carefully all my physical writings or to go into the longer treatises at all, I have myself prepared an epitome of the whole system, Herodotus, to preserve in the memory enough of the principal doctrines, to the end that on every occasion they may be able to aid themselves on the most important points, so far as they take up the study of Physics. Those who have made some advance in the survey of the entire system ought to fix in their minds under the principal headings an elementary outline of the whole treatment of the subject. For a comprehensive view is often required, the details but seldom.

To the former, then—the main heads—we must continually return, and must memorize them so far as to get a valid conception of the facts, as well as the means of discovering all the details exactly when once the general outlines are rightly understood and remembered; since it is the privilege of the mature student to make a ready use of his conceptions by referring every one of them to elementary facts and simple terms. For it is impossible to gather up the results of continuous diligent study of the entirety of things, unless we can embrace in short formulas and hold in mind all that might have been accurately expressed even to the minutest detail.

Hence, since such a course is of service to all who take up natural science, I, who devote to the subject my continuous energy and reap the calm enjoyment of a life like this, have prepared for you just such an epitome and manual of the doctrines as a whole.

In the first place, Herodotus, you must understand what it is that words denote, in order that by reference to this we may be in a position to test opinions, inquiries, or problems, so that our proofs may not run on untested ad infinitum, nor the terms we use be empty of meaning. For the primary signification of every term employed must be clearly seen, and ought to need no proving; this being necessary, if we are to have something to which the point at issue or the problem or the opinion before us can be referred.

Next, we must by all means stick to our sensations, that is, simply to the present impressions whether of the mind or of any criterion whatever, and similarly to our actual feelings, in order that we may have the means of determining that which needs confirmation and that which is obscure.

When this is clearly understood, it is time to consider generally things which are obscure. To begin with, nothing comes into being out of what is non-existent For in that case anything would have arisen out of anything, standing as it would in no need of its proper germs. And if that which disappears had been destroyed and become non-existent, everything would have perished, that into which the things were dissolved being non-existent. Moreover, the sum total of things was always such as it is now, and such it will ever remain. For there is nothing into which it can change. For outside the sum of things there is nothing which could enter into it and bring about the change.

Further, the whole of being consists of bodies and space. For the existence of bodies is everywhere attested by sense itself, and it is upon sensation that reason must rely when it attempts to infer the unknown from the known. And if there were no space (which we call also void and place and intangible nature), bodies would have nothing in which to be and through which to move, as they are plainly seen to move. Beyond bodies and space there is nothing which by mental apprehension or on its analogy we can conceive to exist. When we speak of bodies and space, both are regarded as wholes or separate things, not as the properties or accidents of separate things.

Again, of bodies some are composite, others the elements of which these composite bodies are made. These elements are indivisible and unchangeable, and necessarily so, if things are not all to be destroyed and pass into non-existence, but are to be strong enough to endure when the composite bodies are broken up, because they possess, a solid nature and are incapable of being anywhere or anyhow dissolved. It follows that the first beginnings must be indivisible, corporeal entities.

Again, the sum of things is infinite. For what is finite has an extremity, and the extremity of anything is discerned only by comparison with something else. Now the sum of things is not discerned by comparison with anything else: hence it has no extremity, it has no limit; and, since it has no limit, it must be unlimited or infinite.

Moreover, the sum of things is unlimited both by reason of the multitude of the atoms and the extent of the void. For if the void were infinite and bodies finite, the bodies would not have stayed anywhere but would have been dispersed in their course through the infinite void, not having any supports or counter-checks to send them back on their upward rebound. Again, if the void were finite, the infinity of bodies would not have anywhere to be.

Furthermore, the atoms, which have no void in them—out of which composite bodies arise and into which they are dissolved—vary indefinitely in their shapes; for so many varieties of things as we see could never have arisen out of a recurrence of a definite number of the same shapes. The like atoms of each shape are absolutely infinite; but the variety of shapes, though indefinitely large, is not absolutely infinite.

The atoms are in continual motion through all eternity. Some of them rebound to a considerable distance from each other, while others merely oscillate in one place when they chance to have got entangled or to be enclosed by a mass of other atoms shaped for entangling.

This is because each atom is separated from the rest by void, which is incapable of offering any resistance to the rebound; while it is the solidity of the atom which makes it rebound after a collision, however short the distance to which it rebounds, when it finds itself imprisoned in a mass of entangling atoms. Of all this there is no beginning, since both atoms and void exist from everlasting.

The repetition at such length of all that we are now recalling to mind furnishes an adequate outline for our conception of the nature of things.

Moreover, there is an infinite number of worlds, some like this world, others unlike it. For the atoms being infinite in number, as has just been proved, are borne ever further in their course. For the atoms out of which a world might arise, or by which a world might be formed, have not all been expended on one world or a finite number of worlds, whether like or unlike this one. Hence there will be nothing to hinder an infinity of worlds.

Again, there are outlines or films, which are of the same shape as solid bodies, but of a thinness far exceeding that of any object that we see. For it is not impossible that there should be found in the surrounding air combinations of this kind, materials adapted for expressing the hollowness and thinness of surfaces, and effluxes preserving the same relative position and motion which they had in the solid objects from which they come. To these films we give the name of "images" or "idols." Furthermore, so long as nothing comes in the way to offer resistance, motion through the void accomplishes any imaginable distance in an inconceivably short time. For resistance encountered is the equivalent of slowness, its absence the equivalent of speed.

Not that, if we consider the minute times perceptible by reason alone, the moving body itself arrives at more than one place simultaneously (for this too is inconceivable), although in time perceptible to sense it does arrive simultaneously, however different the point of departure from that conceived by us. For if it changed its direction, that would be equivalent to its meeting with resistance, even if up to that point we allow nothing to impede the rate of its flight. This is an elementary fact which in itself is well worth bearing in mind. In the next place the exceeding thinness of the images is contradicted by none of the facts under our observation. Hence also their velocities are enormous, since they always find a void passage to fit them. Besides, their incessant effluence meets with no resistance or very little, although many atoms, not to say an unlimited number, do at once encounter resistance.

Besides this, remember that the production of the images is as quick as thought. For particles are continually streaming off from the surface of bodies, though no diminution of the bodies is observed, because other particles take their place. And those given off for a long time retain the position and arrangement which their atoms had when they formed part of the solid bodies, although occasionally they are thrown into confusion, Sometimes such films a are formed very rapidly in the air, because they need not have any solid content; and there are other modes in which they may be formed. For there is nothing in all this which is contradicted by sensation, if we in some sort look at the clear evidence of sense, to which we should also refer the continuity of particles in the objects external to ourselves.

We must also consider that it is by the entrance of something coming from external objects that we see their shapes and think of them. For external things would not stamp on us their own nature of color and form through the medium of the air which is between them and use or by means of rays of light or currents of any sort going from us to them, so well as by the entrance into our eyes or minds, to whichever their size is suitable, of certain films coming from the things themselves, these films or outlines being of the same color and shape as the external things themselves. They move with rapid motion; and this again explains why they present the appearance of the single continuous object, and retain the mutual interconnection which they had in the object, when they impinge upon the sense, such impact being due to the oscillation of the atoms in the interior of the solid object from which they come. And whatever presentation we derive by direct contact, whether it be with the mind or with the sense-organs, be it shape that is presented or other properties, this shape as presented is the shape of the solid thing, and it is due either to a close coherence of the image as a whole or to a mere remnant of its parts. Falsehood and error always depend upon the intrusion of opinion when a fact awaits confirmation or the absence of contradiction, which fact is afterwards frequently not confirmed or even contradicted following a certain movement in ourselves connected with, but distinct from, the mental picture presented—which is the cause of error.

For the presentations which, for example, are received in a picture or arise in dreams, or from any other form of apprehension by the mind or by the other criteria of truth, would never have resembled what we call the real and true things, had it not been for certain actual things of the kind with which we come in contact. Error would not have occurred, if we had not experienced some other movement in ourselves, conjoined with, but distinct from, the perception of what is presented. And from this movement, if it be not confirmed or be contradicted, falsehood results; while, if it be confirmed or not contradicted, truth results.

And to this view we must closely adhere, if we are not to repudiate the criteria founded on the clear evidence of sense, nor again to throw all these things into confusion by maintaining falsehood as if it were truth.

Again, hearing takes place when a current passes from the object, whether person or thing, which emits voice or sound or noise, or produces the sensation of hearing in any way whatever. This current is broken up into homogeneous particles, which at the same time preserve a certain mutual connection and a distinctive unity extending to the object which emitted them, and thus, for the most part, cause the perception in that case or, if not, merely indicate the presence of the external object. For without the transmission from the object of a certain interconnection of the parts no such sensation could arise. Therefore we must not suppose that the air itself is molded into shape by the voice emitted or something similar; for it is very far from being the case that the air is acted upon by it in this way. The blow which is struck in us when we utter a sound causes such a displacement of the particles as serves to produce a current resembling breath, and this displacement gives rise to the sensation of hearing.

Again, we must believe that smelling, like hearing, would produce no sensation, were there not particles conveyed from the object which are of the proper sort for exciting the organ of smelling, some of one sort, some of another, some exciting it confusedly and strangely, others quietly and agreeably.

Moreover, we must hold that the atoms in fact possess none of the qualities belonging to things which come under our observation, except shape, weight, and size, and the properties necessarily conjoined with shape. For every quality changes, but the atoms do not change, since, when the composite bodies are dissolved, there must needs be a permanent something, solid and indissoluble, left behind, which makes change possible: not changes into or from the non-existent. but often through differences of arrangement, and sometimes through additions and subtractions of the atoms. Hence these somethings capable of being diversely arranged must be indestructible, exempt from change, but possessed each of its own distinctive mass and configuration. This must remain.

For in the case of changes of configuration within our

experience the figure is supposed to be inherent when other qualities are stripped of, but the qualities are not supposed, like the shape which is left behind, to inhere in the subject of change, but to vanish altogether from the body. Thus, then, what is left behind is sufficient to account for the differences in composite bodies, since something at least must necessarily be left remaining and be immune from annihilation.

Again, you should not suppose that the atoms have any and every size, lest you be contradicted by facts; but differences of size must be admitted; for this addition renders the facts of feeling and sensation easier of explanation. But to attribute any and every magnitude to the atoms does not help to explain the differences of quality in things; moreover, in that case atoms large enough to be seen ought to have reached us, which is never observed to occur; nor can we conceive how its occurrence should be possible, in other words that an atom should become visible.

Besides, you must not suppose that there are parts unlimited in number, be they ever so small, in any finite body. Hence not only must we reject as impossible subdivision ad infinitum into smaller and smaller parts, lest we make all things too weak and, in our conceptions of the aggregates, be driven to pulverize the things that exist, in other words the atoms, and annihilate them; but in dealing with finite things we must also reject as impossible the progression ad infinitum by less and less increments.

For when once we have said that an infinite number of particles, however small, are contained in anything, it is not possible to conceive how it could any longer be limited or finite in size. For clearly our infinite number of particles must have some size; and then, of whatever size they were, the aggregate they made would be infinite. And, in the next place, since what is finite has an extremity which is distinguishable, even if it is not by itself observable, it is not possible to avoid thinking of another such extremity next to this. Nor can we help thinking that in this way, by proceeding forward from one to the next in order, it is possible by such a progression to arrive in thought at infinity.

We must consider the minimum perceptible by sense as not corresponding to that which is capable of being traversed, that is to say is extended, nor again as utterly unlike it, but as having something in common with the things capable of being traversed, though it is without distinction of parts. But when from the illusion created by this common property we think we shall distinguish something in the minimum, one part on one side and another part on the other side, it must be another minimum equal to the first which catches our eye. In fact, we see these minima one after another, beginning with the first, and not as occupying the same space; nor do we see them touch one another's parts with their parts, but we see that by virtue of their own peculiar character (as being unit indivisibles) they afford a means of measuring magnitudes: there are more of them, if the magnitude measured is greater; fewer of them, if the magnitude measured is less.

We must recognize that this analogy also holds of the minimum in the atom; it is only in minuteness that it differs from that which is observed by sense, but it follows the same analogy. On the analogy of things within our experience we have declared that the atom has magnitude; and this, small as it is, we have merely reproduced on a larger scale. And further, the least and simplest things must be regarded as extremities of lengths, furnishing from themselves as units the means of measuring lengths, whether greater or less, the mental vision being employed, since direct observation is impossible. For the community which exists between them and the unchangeable parts (the minimal parts of area or surface) is sufficient to justify the conclusion so far as this goes. But it is not possible that these minima of the atom should group themselves together through the possession of motion.

Further, we must not assert "up" and "down" of that which is unlimited, as if there were a zenith or nadir. As to the space overhead, however, if it be possible to draw a line to infinity from the point where we stand, we know that never will this space—or, for that matter, the space below the supposed standpoint if produced to infinity—appear to us to be at the same time "up" and "down" with reference to the same point; for this is inconceivable. Hence it is possible to assume one direction of motion, which we conceive as extending upwards ad infinitum, and another downwards, even if it should happen ten thousand times that what moves from us to the spaces above our heads reaches the feet of those above us, or that which moves downwards from us the heads of those below us. None the less is it true that the whole of the motion in the respective cases is conceived as extending in opposite directions ad infinitum.

When they are travelling through the void and meet with no resistance, the atoms must move with equal speed. Neither will heavy atoms travel more quickly than small and light ones, so long as nothing meets them, nor will small atoms travel more quickly than large ones, provided they always find a passage suitable to their size. and provided also that they meet with no obstruction. Nor will their upward or their lateral motion, which is due to collisions, nor again their downward motion, due to weight, affect their velocity. As long as either motion obtains, it must continue, quick as the speed of thought, provided there is no obstruction, whether due to external collision or to the atoms' own weight counteracting the force of the blow.

Moreover, when we come to deal with composite bodies, one of them will travel faster than another, although their atoms have equal speed. This is because the atoms in the aggregates are travelling in one direction a during the shortest continuous time, albeit they move in different directions in times so short as to be appreciable only by the reason, but frequently collide until the continuity of their motion is appreciated by sense. For the assumption that beyond the range of direct observation even the minute times conceivable by reason will present continuity of motion is not true in the case before us. Our canon is that direct observation by sense and direct apprehension by the mind are alone invariably true.

Next, keeping in view our perceptions and feelings (for so shall we have the surest grounds for belief), we must recognize generally that the soul is a corporeal thing, composed of fine particles, dispersed all over the frame, most nearly resembling wind with an admixture of heat, in some respects like wind, in others like heat. But, again, there is the third part which exceeds the other two in the fineness of its particles and thereby keeps in closer touch with the rest of the frame. And this is shown by the mental faculties and feelings, by the ease with which the mind moves, and by thoughts, and by all those things the loss of which causes death. Further, we must keep in mind that soul has the greatest share in causing sensation. Still, it would not have had sensation, had it not been somehow confined within the rest of the frame. But the rest of the frame, though it provides this indispensable conditions for the soul, itself also has a share, derived from the soul, of the said quality; and yet does not possess all the qualities of soul. Hence on the departure of the soul it loses sentience. For it had not this power in itself; but something else, congenital with the body, supplied it to body: which other thing, through the potentiality actualized in it by means of motion, at once acquired for itself a quality of sentience, and, in virtue of the neighbourhood and interconnection between them, imparted it (as I said) to the body also.

Hence, so long as the soul is in the body, it never loses sentience through the removal of some other part. The containing sheaths may be dislocated in whole or in part, and portions of the soul may thereby be lost; yet in spite of this the soul, if it manage to survive, will have sentience. But the rest of the frame, whether the whole of it survives or only a part, no longer has sensation, when once those atoms have departed, which, however few in number, are required to constitute the nature of soul. Moreover, when the whole frame is broken up, the soul is scattered and has no longer the same powers as before, nor the same notions; hence it does not possess sentience either.

For we cannot think of it as sentient, except it be in this composite whole and moving with these movements; nor can we so think of it when the sheaths which enclose and surround it are not the same as those in which the soul is now located and in which it performs these movements.

There is the further point to be considered, what the incorporeal can be, if, I mean, according to current usage the term is applied to what can be conceived as self-existent. But it is impossible to conceive anything that is incorporeal as self-existent except empty space. And empty space cannot itself either act or be acted upon, but simply allows body to move through it. Hence those who call soul incorporeal speak foolishly. For if it were so, it could neither act nor be acted upon. But, as it is, both these properties, you see, plainly belong to soul.

If, then, we bring all these arguments concerning soul to the criterion of our feelings and perceptions, and if we keep in mind the proposition stated at the outset, we shall see that the subject has been adequately comprehended in outline: which will enable us to determine the details with accuracy and confidence.

Moreover, shapes and couloirs, magnitudes and weights, and in short all those qualities which are predicated of body, in so far as they are perpetual properties either of all bodies or of visible bodies, are knowable by sensation of these very properties: these, I say, must not be supposed to exist independently by themselves (for that is inconceivable), nor yet to be non-existent, nor to be some other and incorporeal entities cleaving to body, nor again to be parts of body. We must consider the whole body in a general way to derive its permanent nature from all of them, though it is not, as it were, formed by grouping them together in the same way as when from the particles themselves a larger aggregate is made up, whether these particles be primary or any magnitudes whatsoever less than the particular whole. All these qualities, I repeat, merely give the body its own permanent nature. They all have their own characteristic modes of being perceived and distinguished, but always along with the whole body in which they inhere and never in separation from it; and it is in virtue of this complete conception of the body as a whole that it is so designated.

Again, qualities often attach to bodies without being permanent concomitants. They are not to be classed among invisible entities nor are they incorporeal. Hence, using the term "accidents" in the commonest sense, we say plainly that "accidents" have not the nature of the whole thing to which they belong, and to which, conceiving it as a whole, we give the name of body, nor that of the permanent properties without which body cannot be thought of. And in virtue of certain peculiar modes of apprehension into which the complete body always enters, each of them can be called an accident. But only as often as they are seen actually to belong to it, since such accidents are not perpetual concomitants. There is no need to banish from reality this clear evidence that the accident has not the nature of that whole—by us called body—to which it belongs, nor of the permanent properties which accompany the whole. Nor, on the other hand, must we suppose the accident to have independent existence (for this is just as inconceivable in the case of accidents as in that of the permanent properties); but, as is manifest, they should all be regarded as accidents, not as permanent concomitants, of bodies, nor yet as having the rank of independent existence. Rather they are seen to be exactly as and what sensation itself makes them individually claim to be.

There is another thing which we must consider carefully. We must not investigate time as we do the other accidents which we investigate in a subject, namely, by referring them to the preconceptions envisaged in our minds; but we must take into account the plain fact itself, in virtue of which we speak of time as long or short, linking to it in intimate connection this attribute of duration. We need not adopt any fresh terms as preferable, but should employ the usual expressions about it. Nor need we predicate anything else of time, as if this something else contained the same essence as is contained in the proper meaning of the word "time" (for this also is done by some). We must chiefly reflect upon that to which we attach this peculiar character of time, and by which we measure it. No further proof is required: we have only to reflect that we attach the attribute of time to days and nights and their parts, and likewise to feelings of pleasure and pain and to neutral states, to states of movement and states of rest, conceiving a peculiar accident of these to be this very characteristic which we express by the word "time."

After the foregoing we have next to consider that the worlds and every finite aggregate which bears a strong resemblance to things we commonly see have arisen out of the infinite. For all these, whether small or great, have been separated off from special conglomerations of atoms; and all things are again dissolved, some faster, some slower, some through the action of one set of causes, others through the action of another.

And further, we must not suppose that the worlds have necessarily one and the same shape. For nobody can prove that in one sort of world there might not be contained, whereas in another sort of world there could not possibly be, the seeds out of which animals and plants arise and all the rest of the things we see.

Again, we must suppose that nature too has been taught and forced to learn many various lessons by the facts themselves, that reason subsequently develops what it has thus received and makes fresh discoveries, among some tribes more quickly, among others more slowly, the progress thus made being at certain times and seasons greater, at others less.

Hence even the names of things were not originally due to convention, but in the several tribes under the impulse of special feelings and special presentations of sense primitive man uttered special cries. The air thus emitted was molded by their individual feelings or sense-presentations, and differently according to the difference of the regions which the tribes inhabited. Subsequently whole tribes adopted their own special names, in order that their communications might be less ambiguous to each other and more briefly expressed. And as for things not visible, so far as those who were conscious of them tried to introduce any such notion, they put in circulation certain names for them, either sounds which they were instinctively compelled to utter or which they selected by reason on analogy according to the most general cause there can be for expressing oneself in such a way.

Nay more: we are bound to believe that in the sky revolutions, solstices, eclipses, risings and settings, and the like, take place without the ministration or command, either now or in the future, of any being who it the same time enjoys perfect bliss along with immortality. For troubles and anxieties and feelings of anger and partiality do not accord with bliss, but always imply weakness and fear and dependence upon one's neighbours. Nor, again, must we hold that things which are no more than globular masses of fire, being at the same time endowed with bliss, assume these motions at will. Nay, in every term we use we must hold fast to all the majesty which attaches to such notions as bliss and immortality, lest the terms should generate opinions inconsistent with this majesty. Otherwise such inconsistency will of itself suffice to produce the worst disturbance in our minds. Hence, where we find phenomena invariably recurring, the invariability of the recurrence must be ascribed to the original interception and conglomeration of atoms whereby the world was formed.

Further, we must hold that to arrive at accurate knowledge of the cause of things of most moment is the business of natural science, and that happiness depends on this (viz. on the knowledge of celestial and atmospheric phenomena), and upon knowing what the heavenly bodies really are, and any kindred facts contributing to exact knowledge in this respect.

Further, we must recognize on such points as this no plurality of causes or contingency, but must hold that nothing suggestive of conflict or disquiet is compatible with an immortal and blessed nature. And the mind can grasp the absolute truth of this.

But when we come to subjects for special inquiry, there is nothing in the knowledge of risings and settings and solstices and eclipses and all kindred subjects that contributes to our happiness; but those who are well-informed about such matters and yet are ignorant—what the heavenly bodies really are, and what are the most important causes of phenomena, feel quite as much fear as those who have no such special information—nay, perhaps even greater fear, when the curiosity excited by this additional knowledge cannot find a solution or understand the subordination of these phenomena to the highest causes.

Hence, if we discover more than one cause that may account for solstices, settings and risings, eclipses and the like, as we did also in particular matters of detail, we must not suppose that our treatment of these matters fails of accuracy, so far as it is needful to ensure our tranquillity and happiness. When, therefore, we investigate the causes of celestial and atmospheric phenomena, as of all that is unknown, we must take into account the variety of ways in which analogous occurrences happen within our experience; while as for those who do not recognize the difference between what is or comes about from a single cause and that which may be the effect of any one of several causes, overlooking the fact that the objects are only seen at a distance, and are moreover ignorant of the conditions that render, or do not render, peace of mind impossible— all such persons we must treat with contempt. If then we think that an event could happen in one or other particular way out of several, we shall be as tranquil when we recognize that it actually comes about in more ways than one as if we knew that it happens in this particular way.

There is yet one more point to seize, namely, that the greatest ,anxiety of the human mind arises through the belief that the heavenly bodies are blessed and indestructible, and that at the same time they have volition and actions and causality inconsistent with this belief; and through expecting or apprehending some everlasting evil, either because of the myths, or because we are in dread of the mere insensibility of death, as if it had to do with us; and through being reduced to this state not by conviction but by a certain irrational perversity, so that, if men do not set bounds to their terror, they endure as much or even more intense anxiety than the man whose views on these matters are quite vague. But mental tranquillity means being released from all these troubles and cherishing a continual remembrance of the highest and most important truths.

Hence we must attend to present feelings and sense

perceptions, whether those of mankind in general or those peculiar to the individual, and also attend to all the clear evidence available, as given by each of the standards of truth. For by studying them we shall rightly trace to its cause and banish the source of disturbance and dread, accounting for celestial phenomena and for all other things which from time to time befall us and cause the utmost alarm to the rest of mankind.

Here then, Herodotus, you have the chief doctrines of Physics in the form of a summary. So that, if this statement be accurately retained and take effect, a man will, I make no doubt, be incomparably better equipped than his fellows, even if he should never go into all the exact details. For he will clear up for himself many of the points which I have worked out in detail in my complete exposition; and the summary itself, if borne in mind, will be of constant service to him.

It is of such a sort that those who are already tolerably, or even perfectly, well acquainted with the details can, by analysis of what they know into such elementary perceptions as these, best prosecute their researches in physical science as a whole; while those, on the other hand, who are not altogether entitled to rank as mature students can in silent fashion and as quick as thought run over the doctrines most important for their peace of mind.

LETTER TO PYTHOCLES

ABOUT CELESTIAL PHENOMENA AND SCIENTIFIC STUDY

Greetings:

In your letter to me, of which Cleon was the bearer, you continue to show me affection which I have merited by my devotion to you, and you try, not without success, to recall the considerations which make for a happy life. To aid your memory you ask me for a clear and concise statement respecting celestial phenomena; for what we have written on this subject elsewhere is, you tell me, hard to remember, although you have my books constantly with you. I was glad to receive your request and am full of pleasant expectations. We will then complete our writing and grant all you ask. Many others besides you will find these reasonings useful, and especially those who have but recently made acquaintance with the true story of nature and those who are attached to pursuits which go deeper than any part of ordinary education. So you will do well to take and learn them and get them up quickly along with the short epitome in my letter to Herodotus.

In the first place, remember that, like everything else, knowledge of celestial phenomena, whether taken along with other things or in isolation, has no other end in view than peace of mind and firm convictions. We do not seek to wrest by force what is impossible, nor to understand all matters equally well, nor make our treatment always as clear as when we discuss human life or explain the principles of physics in general—for instance, that the whole of being consists of bodies and intangible nature, or that the ultimate elements of things are indivisible, or any other proposition which admits only one explanation of the phenomena to be possible. But this is not the case with celestial phenomena: these at any rate admit of manifold causes for their occurrence and manifold accounts, none of them contradictory of sensation, of their nature.

For in the study of nature we must not conform to empty assumptions and arbitrary laws, but follow the promptings of the facts; for our life has no need now of unreason and false opinion; our one need is untroubled existence. All things go on uninterruptedly, if all be explained by the method of plurality of causes in conformity with the facts, so soon as we duly understand what may be plausibly alleged respecting them. But when we pick and choose among them, rejecting one equally consistent with the phenomena, we clearly fall away from the study of nature altogether and tumble into myth. Some phenomena within our experience afford evidence by which we may interpret what goes on in the heavens. We see bow the former really take place, but not how the celestial phenomena take place, for their occurrence may possibly be due to a variety of causes. However, we must observe each fact as presented, and further separate from it all the facts presented along with it, the occurrence of which from various causes is not contradicted by facts within our experience.

A world is a circumscribed portion of the universe, which contains stars and earth and all other visible things, cut off from the infinite, and terminating in an exterior which may either revolve or be at rest, and be round or triangular or of any other shape whatever. All these alternatives are possible: they are contradicted by none of the facts in this world, in which an extremity can nowhere be discerned.

That there is an infinite number of such worlds can be perceived, and that such a world may arise in a world or in one of the intermundia (by which term we mean the spaces between worlds) in a tolerably empty space and not. as some maintain, in a vast space perfectly clear and void. It arises when certain suitable seeds rush in from a single world or intermundium, or from several, and undergo gradual additions or articulations or changes of place, it may be, and waterings from appropriate sources, until they are matured and firmly settled in so far as the foundations laid can receive them. For it is not enough that there should be an aggregation or a vortex in the empty space in which a world may arise, as the necessitarians hold, and may grow until it collide with another, as one of the so-called physicists says. For this is in conflict with facts.

The sun and moon and the stars generally were not of independent origin and later absorbed, within our world, [such parts of it at least as serve at all for its defence]; but they at once began to take form and grow [and so too did earth and sea] by the accretions and whirling motions of certain substances of finest texture, of the nature either of wind or fire, or of both; for thus sense itself suggests.

The size of the sun and the remaining stars relatively to us is just as great as it appears. But in itself and actually it maybe a little larger or a little smaller, or precisely as great as it is seen to be. For so too fires of which we have experience are seen by sense when we see them at a distance. And every objection brought against this part of the theory will easily be met by anyone who attends to plain facts, as I show in my work On Nature. And the rising and setting of the sun, moon, and stars may be due to kindling and quenching, a provided that the circumstances are such as to produce this result in each of the two regions, east and west: for no fact testifies against this. Or the result might be produced by their coming forward above the earth and again by its intervention to hide them: for no fact testifies against this either. And their motions may be due to the rotation of the whole heaven, or the heaven may be at rest and they alone rotate according to some necessary impulse to rise, implanted at first when the world was made ... and this through excessive heat, due to a certain extension of the fire which always encroaches upon that which is near it.

The turnings of the sun and moon in their course may be due to the obliquity of the heaven, whereby it is forced back at these times. Again, they may equally be due to the contrary pressure of the air or, it may be, to the fact that either the fuel from time to time necessary has been consumed in the vicinity or there is a dearth of it. Or even because such a whirling motion was from the first inherent in these stars so that they move in a sort of spiral. For all such explanations and the like do Dot conflict with any clear evidence, if only in such details we hold fast to what is possible, and can bring each of these explanations into accord with the facts, unmoved by the servile artifices of the astronomers.

The waning of the moon and again her waxing might be due to the rotation of the moon's body, and equally well to configurations which the air assumes; further, it may be due to the interposition of certain bodies. In short, it may happen in any of the ways in which the facts within our experience suggest such an appearance to be explicable. But one must not be so much in love with the explanation by a single way as wrongly to reject all the others from ignorance of what can, and what cannot, be within human knowledge, and consequent longing to discover the undiscoverable. Further, the moon may possibly shine by her own light, just as possibly she may derive her light from the sun; for in our own experience we see many things which shine by their own light and many also which shine by borrowed light. And none of the celestial phenomena stand in the way, if only we always keep in mind the method of plural explanation and the several consistent assumptions and causes, instead of dwelling on what is inconsistent and giving it a false importance so as always to fall back in one way or another upon the single explanation. The appearance of the face in the moon may equally well arise from interchange of parts, or from interposition of something, or in any other of the ways which might be seen to accord with the facts. For in all the celestial phenomena such a line of research is not to be abandoned; for, if you fight against clear evidence, you never can enjoy genuine peace of mind.

An eclipse of the sun or moon may be due to the extinction of their light, just as within our own experience this is observed to happen; and again by interposition of something else—whether it be the earth or some other invisible body like it. And thus we must take in conjunction the explanations which agree with one another, and remember that the concurrence of more than one at the same time may not impossibly happen.

And further, let the regularity of their orbits be

explained in the same way as certain ordinary incidents within our own experience; the divine nature must not on any account be adduced to explain this, but must be kept free from the task and in perfect bliss. Unless this be done, the whole study of celestial phenomena will be in vain, as indeed it has proved to be with some who did not lay hold of a possible method, but fell into the folly of supposing that these events happen in one single way only and of rejecting all the others which are possible, suffering themselves to be carried into the realm of the unintelligible,. and being unable to take a comprehensive view of the facts which must be taken as clues to the rest.

The variations in the length of nights and days may be due to the swiftness and again to the slowness of the sun's motion in the sky, owing to the variations in the length of spaces traversed and to his accomplishing some distances more swiftly or more slowly, as happens sometimes within our own experience; and with these facts our explanation of celestial phenomena must agree; whereas those who adopt only one explanation are in conflict with the facts and are utterly mistaken as to the way in which man can attain knowledge.

The signs in the sky which betoken the weather may be due to mere coincidence of the seasons, as is the case with signs from animals seen on earth, or they may be caused by changes and alterations in the air. For neither the one explanation nor the other is in conflict with facts, and it is not easy to see in which cases the effect is due to one cause or to the other.

Clouds may form and gather either because the air is condensed under the pressure of winds, or because atoms which hold together and are suitable to produce this result become mutually entangled, or because currents collect from tile earth and the waters ; and there are several other ways in which it is not impossible for the aggregations of such bodies into clouds to be brought about. And that being so, rain may be produced from them sometimes by their compression, sometimes by their transformation; or again may be caused by exhalations of moisture rising from suitable places through the air, while a more violent inundation is due to certain accumulations suitable for such discharge. Thunder may be due to the rolling of wind in the hollow parts of the clouds, as it is sometimes imprisoned in vessels which we use; or to the roaring of fire in them when blown by a wind, or to the rending and disruption of clouds, or to the friction and splitting up of clouds when they have become as firm as ice.

As in the whole survey, so in this particular point, the facts invite us to give a plurality of explanations. Lightning too happens in a variety of ways. For when the clouds rub against each other and collide, that collocation of atoms which is the cause of fire generates lightning; or it may be due to the flashing forth from the clouds, by reason of winds, of particles capable of producing this brightness; or else it is squeezed out of the clouds when they have been condensed either by their own action or by that of the winds; or again, the light diffused from the stars may be enclosed in the clouds, then driven about by their motion and by that of the winds, and finally make its escape from the clouds; or light of the finest texture may be filtered through the clouds (whereby the clouds may be set on fire and thunder produced), and the motion of this light may make lightning; or it may arise from the combustion of wind brought about by the violence of its motion and the intensity of its compression; or, when the clouds are rent asunder by winds, and the atoms which generate fire are expelled, these likewise cause lightning to appear.

And it may easily be seen that its occurrence is possible in many other ways, so long as we hold fast to facts and take a general view of what is analogous to them. Lightning precedes thunder, when the clouds are constituted as mentioned above and the configuration which produces lightning is expelled at the moment when the wind falls upon the cloud, and the wind being rolled up afterwards produces the roar of thunder; or, if both are simultaneous, the lightning moves with a greater velocity towards its and the thunder lags behind, exactly as when persons who are striking blows are observed from a distance. A thunderbolt is caused when winds are repeatedly collected, imprisoned, and violently ignited; or when a part is torn asunder and is more violently expelled downwards, the rending being due to the fact that the compression of the clouds has made the neighboring parts more dense; or again it may be due like thunder merely to the expulsion of the imprisoned fire, when this has accumulated and been more violently inflated with wind and has torn the cloud, being unable to withdraw to the adjacent parts because it is continually more and more closely compressed [generally by some high mountain where thunderbolts mostly fall]. And there are several other ways in which thunderbolts may possibly be produced. Exclusion of myth is the sole condition necessary; and it will be excluded, if one properly attends to the facts and hence draws inferences to interpret what is obscure.

Fiery whirlwinds are due to the descent of a cloud forced downwards like a pillar by the wind in full force and carried by a gale round and round, while at the same time the outside wind gives the cloud a lateral thrust; or it may be due to a change of the wind which veers to all points of the compass as a current of air from above helps to force it to move; or it may be that a strong eddy of winds has been started and is unable to burst through laterally because the air around is closely condensed. And when they descend upon land, they cause what are called tornadoes, in accordance with the various ways in which they are produced through the force of the wind; and when let down upon the sea, they cause waterspouts.

Earthquakes may be due to the imprisonment of wind underground, and to its being interspersed with small masses of earth and then set in continuous motion, thus causing the earth to tremble. And the earth either takes in this wind from without or from the falling in of foundations, when undermined, into subterranean caverns, thus raising a wind in the imprisoned air. Or they may be due to the propagation of movement arising from the fall of many foundations and to its being again checked when it encounters the more solid resistance of earth. And there are many other causes to which these oscillations of the earth may be due.

Winds arise from time to time when foreign matter continually and gradually finds its way into the air; also through the gathering of great store of water. The rest of the winds arise when a few of them fall into the many hollows and they are thus divided and multiplied.

Hail is caused by the firmer congelation and complete transformation, and subsequent distribution into drops, of certain particles resembling wind : also by the slighter congelation of certain particles of moisture and the vicinity of certain particles of wind which at one and the same time forces them together and makes them burst, so that they become frozen in parts and in the whole mass. The round shape of hailstones is not impossibly due to the extremities on all sides being melted and to the fact that, as explained, particles either of moisture or of wind surround them evenly on all sides and in every quarter, when they freeze.

Snow may be formed when a fine rain issues from the clouds because the pores are symmetrical and because of the continuous and violent pressure of the winds upon clouds which are suitable; and then this rain has been frozen on its way because of some violent change to coldness in the regions below the clouds. Or again, by congelation in clouds which have uniform density a fall of snow might occur through the clouds which contain moisture being densely packed in close proximity to each other; and these clouds produce a sort of compression and cause hail, and this happens mostly in spring. And when frozen clouds rub against each other., this accumulation of snow might be thrown off. And there are other ways in which snow might be formed.

Dew is formed when such particles as are capable of producing this sort of moisture meet each other from the air: again by their rising from moist and damp places, the sort of place where dew is chiefly formed, and their subsequent coalescence, so as to create moisture and fall downwards, just as in several cases something similar is observed to take place under our eyes. And the formation of hoar-frost is not different from that of dew, certain particles of such a nature becoming in some such way congealed owing to a certain condition of cold air.

Ice is formed by the expulsion from the water of the

circular, and the compression of the scalene and acute-angled atoms contained in it; further by the accretion of such atoms from without, which being driven together cause the water to solidify after the expulsion of a certain number of round atoms.

The rainbow arises when the sun shines upon humid air; or again by a certain peculiar blending of light with air, which will cause either all the distinctive qualities of these colours or else some of them belonging to a single kind, and from the reflection of this light the air all around will be colored as we see it to be, as the sun shines upon its parts. The circular shape which it assumes is due to the fact that the distance of every point is perceived by our sight to be equal; or it may be because, the atoms in the air or in the clouds and deriving from the sun having been thus united, the aggregate of them presents a sort of roundness.

A halo round the moon arises because the air on all sides extends to the moon; or because it equably raises upwards the currents from the moon so high as to impress a circle upon the cloudy mass and not to separate it altogether; or because it raises the air which immediately surrounds the moon symmetrically from all sides up to a circumference round her and there forms a thick ring. And this happens at certain parts either because a current has forced its wry in from without or because the heat has gained possession of certain passages in order to effect this.

Comets arise either because fire is nourished in certain places at certain intervals in the heavens, if circumstances are favourable; or because at times the heaven has a particular motion above us so that such stars appear; or because the stars themselves are set in motion under certain conditions and come to our neighbourhood and show themselves. And their disappearance is due to the causes which are the opposite of these. Certain stars may revolve without setting not only for the reason alleged by some, because this is the part of the world round which, itself unmoved, the rest revolves, but it may also be because a circular eddy of air surrounds this part, which prevents them from travelling out of sight like other stars or because there is a dearth of necessary fuel farther on, while there is abundance in that part where they are seen to be. Moreover there are several other ways in which this might be brought about, as may be seen by anyone capable of reasoning in accordance with the facts.

The wanderings of certain stars, if such wandering is their actual motion, and the regular movement of certain other stars, may be accounted for by saying that they originally moved in a circle and were constrained, some of them to be whirled round with the same uniform rotation and others with a whirling motion which varied; but it may also be that according to the diversity of the regions traversed in some places there are uniform tracts of air, forcing them forward in one direction and burning uniformly, in others these tracts present such irregularities 4s cause the motions observed. To assign a single cause for these effects when the facts suggest several causes is madness and a strange inconsistency; yet it is done by adherents of rash astronomy, who assign meaningless causes for the stars whenever they persist in saddling the divinity with burdensome tasks. That certain stars are seen to be left behind by others may be because they travel more slowly, though they go the same round as the others; or it may be that they are drawn back by the same whirling motion and move in the opposite direction; or again it may be that some travel over a larger and others over a smaller space in making the same revolution. But to lay down as assured a single explanation of these phenomena is worthy of those who seek to dazzle the multitude with marvels.

Falling stars, as they are called, may in some cases be due to the mutual friction of the stars themselves, in other cases to the expulsion of certain parts when that mixture of fire and air takes place which was mentioned when we were discussing lightning; or it may be due to the meeting of atoms capable of generating fire, which accord so well as to produce this result, and their subsequent motion wherever the impulse which brought them together at first leads them; or it may be that wind collects in certain dense mistlike masses and, since it is imprisoned, ignites and then bursts forth upon whatever is round about it, and is carried to that place to which its motion impels it. And there are other ways in which this can be brought about without recourse to myths.

The fact that the weather is sometimes foretold from the behaviour of certain animals is a mere coincidence in time. For the animals offer no necessary reason why a storm should be produced and no divine being sits observing when these animals go out and afterwards fulfilling the signs which they have given. For such folly as this would not possess the most ordinary being if ever so little enlightened, much less one who enjoys perfect felicity.

All this, Pythocles, you should keep in mind; for then you will escape a long way from myth, and you will be able to view in their connection the instances which are similar to these. But above all give yourself up to the study of first principles and of infinity and of kindred subjects, and further of the standards and of the feelings and of the end for which we choose between them. For to study these subjects together will easily enable you to understand the causes of the particular phenomena. And those who have not fully accepted this, in proportion as they have not done so, will be ill acquainted with these very subjects, nor have they secured the end for which they ought to be studied.

LETTER TO IDOMENEUS

EPICURUS WROTE THIS BRIEF NOTE TO A MEMBER OF
HIS SCHOOL WHILE ON HIS DEATH-BED:

On this blissful day, which is also the last of my life, I write this to you. My continual sufferings from strangury and dysentery are so great that nothing could increase them; but I set above them all the gladness of mind at the memory of our past conversations. But I would have you, as becomes your lifelong attitude to me and to philosophy, watch over the children of Metrodorus.

LAST WILL

In this manner I give and bequeath all my property to Amynomachus, son of Philocrates of Bate and Timocrates, son of Demetrius of Potamus, to each severally according to the items of the deed of gift registered in the Metroon, on condition that they shall place the garden and all that pertains to it at the disposal of Hermarchus, son of Agemortus, of Mitylene, and the members of his society, and those whom Hermarchus may leave as his successors, to live and study in. And I entrust to my School in perpetuity the task of aiding Amynomachus and Timocrates and their heirs to preserve to the best of their power the common life in the garden in whatever way is best, and that these may help to maintain the garden in the same way as those to whom our successors in the School may bequeath it. And let Amynomachus and Timocrates permit Hermarchus and his associates to live in the house in Melite for the lifetime of Hermarchus.

And from the revenues made over by me to Amynomachus and Timocrates let them to the best of their power in consultation with Hermarchus make separate provision for the funeral offerings to my father, mother, and brothers, and for the customary celebration of my birthday on the tenth day of Gamelion in each year, and for the meeting of all my School held every month on the twentieth day to commemorate Metrodorus and myself according to the rules now in force. Let them also join in celebrating the day in Poseideon which commemorates my brothers, and likewise the day in Metageitnion which commemorates Polyaenus, as I have done previously.

And let Amynomachus and Timocrates take care of Epicurus, the son of Metrodorus, and of the son of Polyaenus, so long as they study and live with Hermarchus. Let them likewise provide for he maintenance of Metrodorus's daughters so long as she is well-ordered and obedient to Hermarchus; and, when she comes of age, give her in marriage to a husband selected by Hermarchus from among the members of the School; and out of the revenues accruing to me let Amynomachus and Timocrates in consultation with Hermarchus give to them as much as they think proper for their maintenance year by year.

Let them make Hermarchus trustee of the funds along with themselves, in order that everything may be done in concert with him, who has grown old with me in philosophy and is left at the head of the School. And when the girl comes of age, let Amynomachus and Timocrates pay her dowry, taking from the property as much as circumstances allow, subject to the approval of Hermarchus. Let them provide for Nicanor as I have done previously, so that none of those members of the school who have rendered service to me in private life and have shown me kindness in every way and have chosen to grow old with me in the School should, so far as my means go, lack the necessaries of life.

All my books to be given to Hermarchus.

And if anything should happen to Hermarchus before the children of Metrodorus grow up, Amynomachus and Timocrates shall give from the funds bequeathed by me, so far as possible, enough for their several needs, as long as they are well ordered. And let them provide for the rest according to my arrangements; that everything may be carried out, so far as it lies in their power. Of my slaves I manumit Mys, Nicias, Lycon, and I also give Phaedrium her liberty.